LANGUAGES

Also by Gary Allen

Irish Notes (KT Publications, 1995)
The Farthest Circle (KT Publications, 1996)
Mending Churches (Lapwing Publications, 1997)
Making Waves (Flarestack Publishing, 1997)

LANGUAGES

Gary Allen

The Black Mountain Press

Acknowledgements

Some of these poems have appeared in the following publications:
*Acumen, Ambit, Black Mountain Review, Chapman, The Devil,
Force 10, Fortnight, Honest Ulsterman, London Magazine,
Magma, New Welsh Review, The North, Orbis, Other Poetry,
Poetry Ireland Review, The Reader, Scintilla, Smiths Knoll,
Stand, Tears in the Fence, Thumbscrew, The Wide Skirt.*

First published in the UK in 2002 by Flambard Press
Stable Cottage, East Fourstones, Hexham NE47 5DX
and Black Mountain Press
PO Box 9, Ballyclare, Northern Ireland BT39 0JW

Typeset by Harry Novak
Cover design by Gainford Design Associates
Front cover image: detail from a painting by Noël Shaw
Printed in England by Cromwell Press, Trowbridge, Wiltshire

A CIP catalogue record for this book
is available from the British Library.
ISBN 1 873226 57 8
© 2002 Gary Allen
All rights reserved

Flambard Press wishes to thank Northern Arts
for its financial support.

The publishers wish to thank the Arts Council of Northern Ireland
for financially supporting this publication.

Website: www.flambardpress.co.uk

Contents

Thou Great Redeemer	7
Benediction	8
Above Wageningen	9
Sand	10
Song of Job	11
The Rock	12
Hymnal	13
The Saviour	14
At Helen's Bay	15
The Backs	16
Sisyphus	17
Decay	18
Legends	19
First Love	20
Islands	21
Cock Crow	22
Mirage	24
The Fire-Eaters	25
The Cabinet Maker	26
Germinate	27
The Hireling	28
Miracles	30
The Potato Pickers	32
The Calling	33
The Broiler House	34
Sparks	35
Highland	36
Two Sisters	37
Passage	38
Languages	39

Beyond Liscannor	40
Linen	41
Skin	42
A Scientific Study	43
Preservation	44
Discoveries	45
Mythologies	46
Working Dogs	47
Anthropology	48
The North	49
Transfiguration	50
A Quiet Place	52
Down Under	53
White Horse, Early Morning	54
Stone	55
In a Bombed Hotel in Portstewart	56
Crossing	57
Return to Galway	58
Clabber Street	59
Contrition	60
Thoughts on Armistice Day	61
Born Again	62
Testament	63

Thou Great Redeemer

Cennick came North from Dublin
to preach this muddy acre –

showered with stones and dead dogs.

This field older than the word –
a burial grove of female organs.

We first had sex here –
and I lied about everything,

the eye, childhood-dead and unforgiving,
saw corruption in the promise.

I lost her in the house
of the single men and women,

an unsung stranger
on the road to Wetteravia

seeking truth and redemption
in the nature of birth.

A great aunt went mad with God –
from the bare cell chanted,

When all things else decay,

and died, having carried for sixty years
a calcified child in her uterus.

Benediction

What do you know of love?
it has no name in poverty.

And only the dead talk now –
of shame

blessings that are hidden

voices clear
though the flesh is putrid.

Father unbending in faith

and a late husband, in name
a man unreal

like all men
retaining mystery in dominance

hearing only blame.

In the house of the priest's parents
you blackleaded in a room

full of Africa, with hands of blood:

he went to serve Jesus in Quincy
and his father in his God's pride

locked the door

destroyer of children
with the words,

Work is love made visible.

Above Wageningen

It was hard going
working our way up the firebreaks
pushing wheels against root and branch
swiping away midge and fly.

And the silence up here,
away from the forest road
as I wait, holding the bicycles
while you squat among the ferns.

You are lying on the grass, eyes closed
surrounded by crumpled tinfoil and orange peel
empty bottle of whiskey.

Earlier we had walked among the pines
droplets of sunlight reaching the earthen floor,

and I think of that other time in Ireland
on the farthest slope of Slemish
the sudden appearance of an army helicopter
that came round again before we had finished dressing.

After all these years, you still have nightmares
your mother coming to you, pulling your hair:
the lonely death of an alcoholic.

Below me the Rhine curls silver: it is getting late
the sun falling back among the trees
and the rising breeze blowing cool.

Sand

Here we find ourselves out of season by twenty years:
the lights have gone out at Runkerry House
planks of wood nailed across the windows and doors.

Down the empty side streets, the shabby backs of B&Bs
the air is heavy with salt and chip-shop grease:
young waitresses smoke and wave.

You say if you listen to the wind coming off the seafront,
once again you hear someone shift the keys of a saxophone
from the Arcadia Ballroom on its granite promontory.

Are you still the girl who jammed a chair against the hotel-room door
then sitting on the bed unhooked your bra?
now we watch the young bathers by the harbour wall.

And so it has become too far to walk to the end of the Curran:
these are the small things of life
like the middle-aged men in the dune grass
on the edge of the golf course with their binoculars.

Then stopping, you tell me how as a child
on summer boat trips out to the Skerries
you secretly loved the smaller islands.

Song of Job

Men pray from windows
that light prevails

in the coming darkness,

waves are seen on isolated shores,
and men make prophesies happen.

Suffering is redemptive,
the train wheels chant

the sum of its years as nothing
to the number of lies

a man will tell himself
as he listens.

Father, hard work separates us
from a dull end

our hands are open
though we no longer hunger at the feast

only, let each of us find his meaning:

one man dreams an island in concrete,
this one a love not formed.

And let us not be forgotten
at this hour before rest,

the sleepers on the track answering,
amen, amen, amen.

The Rock

Here father
are all the burned homeworks,

ancient dust
settling on grey washing lines

in grey estates.

Every picture holds a dead face,
from here to Cairo

and the back streets,

bare feet drumming
on the Spinning Mill boards.

This is a door I cannot open –

the poverty of words on paper,
never spoken, nor understood

but handed on in bitterness.

It is the rock I hang from,
and death redeems neither of us.

Hymnal

Now I understand, grandfather
the thickening in my fingers and wrists,

and the silence.

Jesus hangs on every wall
to remind us

of sin, and retribution.

Life leaves by the eyes,
my grandmother said

standing over you in resignation.

And I fear too:
the violent single sound of a phone

that rings and stops
in that hour before rising

in a house that is empty with yourself.

Father, what is the meaning of this cross?
let me walk beyond the garden of Gethsemane

and reject the earth, and what is dust
for the assurance of flesh.

The Saviour

No fisherman would have taken this boat to even calm waters,
the hull bottom a sturdy man could put his foot through in places,
pitch worn like the threadbare coats of those tramping the ditches.

And a good fisherman he had been – in his father's boat
he had rode the white-tipped waves of Tory Sound,
pulled oar and net till his hands turned hard between islands.

He knew the tides of the bays and loughs
could talk weather with seaweed, seal, bird, and star,
judge his own likely fate in the face of swell and fog.

And that night, when the roof of the workhouse was taken away –
joists, beams, picked clean like the ribs of an ocean whale –
he ordered the sick down to the boat, and the safety of the other shore.

And many wailed, in fear of the thunderous roar of wind and water,
laid head to foot, faces covered from the peppering rain with shawls,
weak hands fought to hold the rough hewed oars.

The naked emaciated boy washed in with the morning cold
and the splintered wood, was carried in a hammock of meal sacks
to the crofts under Slieve Snaght,

he told of the boat being steered out to the open sea
and how, as they went under the black walloping waves,
the man at the helm had rejoiced in riotous singing.

At Helen's Bay

It comes to this, the one instant,
the wind-wet pilgrimage with newspaper
from promenade to retirement home:

and age is a plateau of small acceptances.

These man-made walls, with their canteen dinners
and medicine smells, contain the images
of all our fears –

what it is to finally let go.

It is the trivial we return to on real days –

a deep-rooted coppice of glen pine
on a forgotten road long ago:

the undressing and the naked flesh.

Or the disused graveyard at Liminary –
we stalled the engine, killed the lights,
and coasted along,

secure in the vacuum of years not lived.

The Backs

This world is lost to us,
redeveloped in the mind,

and on the ground:

water seeping down black brick
at the back of the timber yard.

It's what we find without thinking –
the breathless games of flesh

that remain smell
(nettle, hedge, earth, urine)

religion defiled,
the crossing of a divide.

Innocence is hard to shock –
we held still like the evening

while they did it against the swinging gate
and she wiped the come from her skirt.

What we observed with wonder,
we now judge and fear –

the man with the executioner's hood
evaporating like the sharp sound of years.

Sisyphus

I first tasted stone as a child,
carrying club money in the wrong estate.

Brought up in the truth,
I gave my religion in innocence.

Stone is never forgotten,
the selection and the throwing is ritual

with the breaking of bone, the cutting of hair:
we love the death we have given.

Those women on the Maiden City wall
hurling stone at history

were only responding to fear.

It is how we fall,
the thickness of a coin.

In that Mexican summer
while others sweltered by television sets,

I dribbled round
the husks of burning cars

marking myself for persecution
by gracing the only house with broken windows.

Decay

This gravel path, unreal and white
lies too straight between the bog,
the drainage ditch, the thickly planted pines:

you would have heard them play on one another –
like ball bearings in a sock.

No one lives up here now,
stone walls falling slowly in upon themselves,
like headstones in an old graveyard
in Brooklyn or Quincy –

or a housing estate in Twinbrook.

And water – dripping through the forest
seeping up to fill footprints,
runned off into Quolie Reservoir

to fill this bath below.

Everything rots on the highland –
primeval wood, sheep carcass, twists of rope.

Legends

We had our Gods too –
domiciled warriors

whose great metal heads
swung slowly between sky and lough.

It rains iron here –
nuts, bolts, rivets,

and men's singlets ripped open
in search of false Gods –

baptism in a shared water.

We offered our sweat too –
Mackies, Sirocco,

a giant's ring of girders
and a drum of rope.

Vengeance is mine says the Lord,
on a warehouse roof,

and you who kill your sons and daughters
look now –

each day this woman
comes searching from the West

on a rumour that a body is buried
where the gulls reel over reclaimed land

and the refuse lorries
tip and plough their rubbish.

First Love

In my house, chairs stood against the windows:
I sweated in fear of the man
with a pillowcase over his head.

The night I walked you home,
lads smoking in the shadows
at the gates of the Parochial House –

Go no farther love, you whispered:

a fool youth, in my rut I would have kissed
you under the famine wall.

And my father sprung up
from the locks he was mending
pressing the blade of a screwdriver to my throat,

his eyes burning like Abraham's.

Love changes nothing, you said,
not even bales of shorn hair,
hillocks of broken teeth.

Islands

You always rowed too close to the islands
afraid of being so far
out in the lough.

Once I spent an afternoon
up to my waist
in cold black water

pulling us free of the reeds
while you sat on the bank
and laughed.

The stone face on Boa Island –
you licked your finger
from the hollow of a head

said you could taste blood:
as the evening cooled you became frightened
hearing voices in the wind.

You would not have chosen
this room yourself
facing away from the water,

fingers playing with the crucifix
you found on Devenish
though you were no longer a Catholic.

Cock Crow

The Last Supper hung
on the whitewashed wall above their bed

a wedding gift
from a shipyard worker to a mill girl

(shilling bought
from a Belfast house clearance).

Those who live with wood
learn to work the grain:

my grandfather's tools
heavy with inheritance

split handles bound with tape
chipped blades,

I believed them sacred
whetted with blood –

self-inflicted wounds,
the smashed bone of strikebreakers from the South.

My grandmother blind in one eye
(a loose spindle)

she kept house in silence
while he prayed in the room above

and I mowed down nettles
on the dung heap

to the sound of the black cockerel
in the chicken run,

and the prominence of the midday sun
blazing like hellfire –

a carpenter's muscular body
at the wrong window.

Mirage

He is dead,
having rubbed like a grain of sand
through the early forties.

Barefoot at thirteen
in the spinning mill,
knew all the scams –

like I learned to manipulate words.

Suspicious of motives, he hated everyone,

the Arabs he was cast among,
he despised without questioning –

and we were Arabs too,

rankling like a dry watercourse
or the awkwardness of a marriage bed.

There is no intimacy with the half-naked boy
sweating on the concrete rim
of an Egyptian reservoir

found at the back of the bureau –

moving across my mind
like formless whispering sand dunes.

The Fire-Eaters

I am a non-person,
subletting your stepfather's apartment,
an internal exile form tribal madness.

At night, the city searchlights
illuminate the taut electric cables from pylons
straddling the veld of the Rhine.

Coming back from the postkantoor in the afternoons
I meet the prostitute cycling down to the stop
to protect her mixed-race daughter getting off the school bus –

she greets me in her Surinam tongue,
a mouth smiling with glistening lipstick:

and dark skin no longer jars in rural Ireland.

Letters from Windhoek, Pretoria, Pietermaritzburg,
delivered through the dirty snow piled outside,
clatter like buckshot in the hall,
pleading with you to get in touch.

A car rests its axles on bricks,
slashed tyres necklacing the shrubs,

and junkies squat for shelter in the broken lift
shouting truth from needles.

In the kitchenette, a collage pinned to the notice board –
newspaper clippings, business cards, photographs,

familiar faces that I can't quite place,
in ritual regalia, with petrol bombs and stones,

caught in sunlight from the open door of a school mud hut.

The Cabinet Maker

And there you are again, the air thick with dust, the smell of fresh
    cut wood,
shavings curling up your muscular tattooed arms as you cut true –
with the breaker and the iron just right –
the odds and ends of rough planks bartered from the timber yard.

A pot of melted, foul-smelling animal glue on the hearth
and old canvas awnings from the lorry depot covering the floor.

You are lost in these hours as never before
excelling in you strength and discipline,
intuition, skilful fingers, that something in the eye
that taught to tease out the wood, the grain, the precise cut

as you slot dovetail, bevel with a spokeshave and file
and with the small knife you fashioned from the iron in the shipyard

inwardly carve the bone-hard handle for a cabinet door,
consoles for shelves, little catches –
the simple beauty of a drawer with its own whisper and light movement.

Germinate

These blue-veined angry hands
(as yet without responsibility)
could be a murderer's, the midwife said

making my exhausted mother cry
under a dune of secondhand birth blankets
and the rough of my father's greatcoat

(that I still like to imagine
contained minute grains of sand
from a Palestine desert in the seams).

And the walls and windows filmed with ice:

my father went out that morning
to beg the loan of a small electric fire,

won at the horses and got drunk
bought three hotwater bottles from a hardware store

and missed me coming: in the blizzard,
all the new council houses looked the same.

Later, when the first paving stones were thrown
she took my father's souvenir handgun

carefully wrapped it in old newspaper
before placing it at the bottom of the rubbish bin.

These hands are adult now
scarred and coloured like my father's at this age,

have carried the coffins of family and friends,

yet have not killed, nor mixed fertilizers,
having neutralized hatred with words.

The Hireling

This is not the house where I was born,
yet could have been,

and round about, the poor fields of bog and stone
wasted with the slaughter of our futures,

the sacrificial mark of flint and iron –
these living-room walls riddled with holes.

Rusting farm implements in the long grass
and pieces of torn dress pinned to the hawthorns,

crows gathered in the barren fields,

and my father's vaguely familiar face
grave through the overgrown branches at the broken pane

warns vainly against love or continuation:

the small bleached bones he dug out
of the peat bank in the Glarryford moss –

the hidden shame of some Sligo skivvy.

He worked out his youth here
eating his piece under hedges,

and once a year, the farmer's wife
bought a hot meal to the kitchen door.

In the Blitz, she gave refuge
to a slum family from Belfast,

the children awed by the inside toilet,
used a corner of the room.

Now the building is without plumbing or porcelain,

and my father spent the last six months of life
tallying harvests, faggots of wood, the cost of seedling,

from his deathbed in a rundown council house.

Miracles

A cold room in a late month:
the light is falling away from the girl
with the dyed black hair

washing her breasts and thighs
at a stained sink with faulty taps.

Supper at the Amsterdam Hilton
with an Iranian businessman

(she feels sorry for the young waiter).

There is no contradiction in our faith:
I knew the scriptures from grandparents
long before I could decipher names

from the gilded pages of the family Bible
my father stole from Palestine in forty-six.

And she was a thin child of the Dutch Reformed Church
touching herself through the pockets of her wide skirt.

An ugly mouth from a botched organisation,
impeding words as harshly as torn skin:

opening herself with the fingers of both hands
charging the younger boys 25c for a look

a backward view of crows falling
like black snow on bare branches
while they abused her with sticks,

the earth frozen under a numb spine.

And all the heavy words of our prophets
could keep neither of us
from the thin pointed truth of needles:

some months before confinement
we talked of miracles –

that morning in the hallway,
the unborn part between her legs,

and believing she understood the nature of things.

The Potato Pickers

My mother gathered potatoes
in the stony field of the Cross,

a smiling child in pigtails
swinging her bare feet over the tailgate,

groping through the dark soil
of furrows sloping up to rock

(in summer, the farmer preached here too,
a layman strong on adultery).

The lumpy potato bread tasting of earth:
she helped his mute wife carry food

to the itinerant workers from the West
who spoke in tongues my mother couldn't understand.

A shilling, and a sack of small potatoes –
and then there was no more work.

My mother said the world turned black
on the day a murderer was being hanged

thirty miles away at the Crumlin.

The Calling

Finger-smoothed copper of a dead Queen
thrown into an upturned coat spread out
on a rough stubbled field,

the first light silvering beaded dew
on grubby Knaves and Kings,

and a voice speaks to my grandfather
of the stillness in the house

ashes turned grey in the morning cold.

A white horse followed him
as he walked across the fields,

and a voice speaks at the crossroads,
I am the Resurrection and the Light.

He cycles thirty miles to Belfast
to fit out ocean liners,

weekly lodgings in Sandy Row,

and the voice speaks again,
I am the unborn, the sword of Flanders.

The Broiler House

She is the fresh one
at the end of this line

of worn-out women with podgy faces
and brawny arms

hands viscid
with guts, giblets, membranes.

The heavy-set man behind them
in the blood-flecked apron
is mouthing a dirty joke,

cleaver-raping moribund meat,
pink and gaping like an open mouth.

This is the beginning of seven children
and the loss of small things –

girlhood, innocence, church on Sunday,
the sanctity of flesh.

Sparks

He worked as a welder
in the shipyard

saw men beaten-up,
thrown into the lough.

After the first raid
a list was made

of which docks, warehouses, factories
had not been hit

the information cycled South –
and then the second raid:

at the bottom of the yard
he serenely watched

the red glow over Belfast
thirty miles away.

Highland

From here on Slievenanee
the land looks like contours on a map,
brown and green
merging to become mountains.

And over there
Carncormick, Collin Top
the rock nipple of Slemish.

It is the North European way
to go naked under the sun
yet you did not allow
for the biting midges

the black bog
oozing soft and cold
between your toes.

What paths there are
you have abandoned long ago
picking your way up the firebreaks
between wedges of forest.

And the look of disbelief
on the young peatcutter's face
as he watches you walk
brown-skinned, bare-breasted
from the pines.

Two Sisters

They never married, seldom left the house:
their father shot for cowardice in a muddy field in France,
the mother died of grief.

We would never play near their yard
kept to the leafy allotments farther down the row
only sometimes daring to chuck half-bricks
at their back door from a distance.

The pigeon men on their hunkers smoking butts
cracked smutty jokes about the sisters
as they waited for the birds coming in from Arklow.

The older sister died on the stairs
when a heart, already scarred, burst open –
the other sister's scream brought neighbours in.

On the day of her sister's burial
she watched from the lifted curtain of a room upstairs –
the women of the street came away from the closed door
still carrying plates of sandwiches and cake.

It was the coalman who found her –
looking through the back window
he saw the crazed cats jump from the table
and cling from the hanging corpse to feed.

Passage

The crossing was rough –
she spent most of it being sick.

The morning air was cold on deck –
the ferry moved slowly into Liverpool docks.

Some cropped-headed tinker boys
were throwing slices of apple to the seagulls,

their sister stood tight against the rail
the wind blowing in the folds of her confirmation dress.

In her bag was a letter from a boy in Gortin
(the big handwriting of a farm labourer,

he wrote of the sea at Castlerock
and the sand dunes at Magilligan)

a cheap nightdress from Wellworth's in Omagh,
a telephone number for Belfast,

and an appointment card
for a clinic in Manchester.

Languages

And this is your first real sense of freedom,
flying down the Alp passes on your Norton into Italy
the flight jacket zipped tight against the wind –
those late-night letters becoming harder to scribble
knowing how heavy every word became in their hands.

The virtues of a good upbringing and self-respect
that your father tried to impart on that last walk along Tremadog Bay,
as you stared at the creased skin on his face and neck
tattooed blue by years at the coalface,
are the very things you hurled your youth against
in the bars and brothels of postwar Berlin.

Visits back to the terraced house in Porthmadog becoming rarer
your dress uniform making you awkward among friends
how you itched to get overseas again
away from uncles, aunts, the solemn chapel Sundays
the rain falling off slates, shop signs, doorways
like the haemorrhaging hours of childhood –
tracing routes along the marble fireplace.

And you could never understand how a man who spent his life in mines
could waste hours studying the texts of your old school grammars –
what Welsh you had flattened out to control-tower monotone
as you talked down combat aircraft over German skies.

His shape still living in the old coat hanging behind the bedroom door,
photographs of himself outside pits in the Rhondda during the forties
scattered with pictures of you on the dresser,
and all the postcards you forgot sending while on leave across Europe.

Beyond Liscannor

And is the light from Loop Head
still silvering the waves at Spanish point?

How long since we walked that strand?
toes popping the air sacs of Frond,

the sea breaking cold upon us,
wrack like fingers wrapping around our ankles,

and the silence –
the first grey light coming from the West.

You began a name of shell, pebble, driftwood
that came to nothing

while I judged the remoteness
of Slieve Elva, Slieve Callan,

and the volume of dark saltwater
between here and the other shore.

Linen

My grandmother started in the spinning room
when she was eleven years old,
suffered badly from the odour of oil and flax.

Under the North light from the saw-edged roof
she worked from six-thirty to six,
the floors vibrating as the heavy shuttles
thundered across the power looms.

And the excessive temperature, spray from the spindles
the deafening noise from whirling power belts
clashing Jacquard cards, banging sleys.

Young boys spitting up blood
after combing the tow from the line,
and the stink of yarn
dressed with carrageen moss, flour and tallow.

You had to be quick on the whistle
to doff bobbins of spun yarn on oiled flyers,
or a whack with a rod across the knuckles.

When she got an infection
from standing barefoot in the contaminated water,
they had to wrench out the entire root
of the great toenail, leaving her with a limp.

And a best friend who fainted with hunger
had her hair entangled in the carding machinery –
lost the greater part of her scalp.

Now they are knocking the old building down
the iron ball turning the small brick to dust,
and I remember as a child, how on passing
she always spat at the chained gate.

Skin

This morning, the forester's cottage looks empty
shutters down, sodden shirts hanging on the line.

The logs are still smouldering from last night's fire
chicken bones, soggy bread, empty beer bottles dotting the grass.

Now we are lost, the coloured lines on the map
failing to show paths blocked by fallen trees.

You follow reluctantly as I pick a way along the waterfalls,
not wanting to see another Neolithic site
sitting out on bare rock or boggy ground on the highland.

And so I give in, lead us out of the forest into the grey light:
a lone donkey is in a field by the side of the road
its hoofs overgrown and split, making it lame.

You shoo away the thick of flies
eating into the open sores around its eyes,
slowly stroke its rough hide muzzle.

Your pity giving way to something silent
as you stare at the black erection
swaying close to its swollen belly.

We don't speak on the way back
the steady drizzle beating the anoraks close to our skins
and the sound of thunder booming down the glen.

A Scientific Study

The men's naked bodies ritually scarred
the septum of the nose pierced
by a small kangaroo bone,
circumcision, evidence of tooth evulsion.

Girls have sex from an early age,
sometimes with more than one male:
the effects of syphilis caught from convicts
is disturbing, many have lost noses.

And they are dying of smallpox in great numbers:
we saw no canoe coming up the harbour
the only natives, those lying dead upon its shores.

Bodies found all over the settlement
dead children lying close, some in the act
of crawling from caves to fresh runs of water:

thank God, I brought with me
variolous material to vaccinate the Europeans.

The skeletons I boil for several hours
in caustic potash to remove the flesh,
the bones labelled and put in bags.

And some skulls sent back
with the flesh intact:
soaked in corrosive sublimate,
then set out to dry,

they become as hard as wood,
the facial forms preserved
without attracting insects.

Preservation

Driving in fencing posts
I see across the valley
can imagine Miliuc looking out
from his rock on Skerry.

I repair drystone walls
sometimes using the hewed stone
from fallen cairns.

And once, cutting out a ditch
found an elaborate souterrain,
the bones of thirty.

O'Neill, the farmer, cursed
about wasters from Queen's,
wanted me to fill it in.

History, he said,
is in the land,
not found behind glass cases.

Discoveries

Rathlin Island,
a grey question mark
sitting in the sea,

and beyond,
the humped Mull of Kintyre.

First sex,
a girl from the campsite,
in the cathedral quietness,

the smell of pine,
in an ancient forest
of carved pagan faces,

the pine cones uncomfortable
beneath her back.

And in the Layd graveyard
where we went to smoke,

scratch our names in the crypt
of the disused church,

we watched the exhumation
of a Spaniard
with sword and helmet.

Mythologies

I liked to wander off on my own
hours passed reading books
on a summerseat along the clifftop path –

Cuchulain, the Tain Bo Cualnge:
the sun sparkling on the sea was Tir na n-Og.

From the pebbled beaches
I climbed through the cool pines
the mountain bog and brown lough

tonguing each Gaelic name place
like the hard stone of a chambered grave.

I played football with local boys
on the hurley pitch

as the light faded, we smoked Woodbines
talked of heroes

till an older boy said
they were not my stories – I was a planter:

and then I understood the strong fingers
of Dunluce, Kinbane, Dunineny.

Working Dogs

We were lucky to get the plastering finished –
as smooth as slate.

I quickly learned not to sub him
till the working day was ended

and drove over each morning
to collect him at his gate

his dogs skiting excitedly
in the cobbled farmyard –

he pointed out two pups
said they weren't worth a curse.

Once on checking, he showed me a favour he had done –
a large rat with its skull trowel-flattened.

In front of me he knocked the pups
from the nest

squelched each one beneath his heel
as though they were rotten spuds.

I met him late one summer evening
the shotgun slung open in the crook of his arm

the two young collies falling over each other
as they ran in front to the moss.

Anthropology

The box came in the morning post
marked airmail – Yucatán,
she lifted out the polished bones
spread them carefully on the table

each fragment tacked and labelled
bits of skull, fibula, tibia, scapular.

As a child on the strand at Downhill
she would take home skeletons of birds
in her duffle-coat pockets
bleaching them in boiling saltwater –

these bones had weathered clean with time:
some had deep cuts on them
neat holes in the cranium plates –
smaller parts were animal.

They wouldn't let her see her son's body
identified him by his teeth:

and in the drinking clubs of West Belfast
they pass around for fun
the stolen pictures of autopsies.

The North

Mine cursed the mills and factories
(not theirs, the stony fields of undersized potatoes)

three generations of slaves, sucked form the crofts
homespun weavers of Slaght, Tully, Lisnamurrikin

packed into the back-to-back slums of Mill Row
cobbles awash with piss, shit, and spilled porter
bobbies patrolling in threes under the hiss of gas lamps,

or coming with carbines to smash doors, furniture, heads,
of those evicted, too sick to work,
snivelling families broken-up and sent to the workhouses.

And still they came, from the hunger in the West
moths to the thud of power looms, breathless humidity, diseased lungs
to the tall chimneys and brick edifices

girdling the banks and races of a poisoned river
(boys bathing naked in the frothy mouths of open sewers)

for low wages that fell and fell with wars and cheap imports:
skulls sliced outside the closed factory gates,
nearing starvation, they went back for less.

And a great uncle in a wooden tower like a sun-god
watching the bleach-greens white with the linen
for the genteel dining rooms of Boston and Philadelphia.

Transfiguration

1

Barely ten years old
I first felt the vibration
of the window glass,
the deep shudder
of the earth.

We rushed to look out
at the spiralling black smoke
rising above the slated rooftops
of the council estate
from the town centre.

Watched as angry men
hurdled the garden hedges
and ran across the greens
looking for vengeance.

Listened to the clang
and wail of bells
and sirens:
for a few moments
we were a whole family.

2

Held back by tape strung
across the road, we watched
and smiled to one another
at the rubbled street
the wreckage of Patterson's
where only the morning before
we had queued unserved among adults:
divine retribution.

3

Johnny Mullan's mother
couldn't get out
of the small boutique
where she worked.

Fire and heat
kept her from the door,
she made her way through
the smoke to the back
of the shop
where she crouched.

We were allowed
to stay home
from school
to go to her funeral.

In his suit,
at the head
of the procession,
he looked different,
almost holy.

A Quiet Place

Early evening
echoing gunshots
distant mountains:
fingers held up to them
like voices –
the last children playing
on the street.

Hard cow dung from yesterday
furrowing the narrow
road:
touched by an early frost
clear as an eye –
a circle of nothing, like blood
on the soil.

Crumpled like a sack
all but naked
silent:
hands tied behind back
head hooded –
this morning, the school bus will go
a different way.

Down Under

At school, they showed us black and white trade films:
men in wide hats, sleeves rolled high above biceps,
on horseback, driving flocks of sheep in Queensland,

smiling with white teeth, in singlets dark with sweat,
holding sheep between their knees, the buzz of shears
as they clipped the wool, easy as blowing away thistledown.

Fruit-canning factories in Adelaide,
mineral quarries in the Northern Territory,
coalmining, and a smelting foundry at Newcastle.

And those fast-moving films of postwar children
with battered suitcases coming solemnly
down the gangways of great ocean liners.

My uncle went out in forty-seven, worked the bus routes,
North from Wynyard Park: South, East, and West
from Circular Quay – cheap bedsits in Kings Cross,
The Rocks, then farther out in Paddington.

In history, we followed Eyre's epic journey
along the Great Australian Bight,
the Aboriginal guides keeping the party alive,
draining roots for water, spearing stingrays for food:

my uncle would have gone no farther than The Gap,
the horses at Randwick or Canterbury, greyhound racing
at Wentworth Park, and the only Aboriginal he knew
was the man he made fun of, who swept the bar.

He never sent letters back to Ireland, said his schooling
hadn't been good: when he died, soaked in whiskey,
he left a stained suit, new set of teeth, one hundred
Australian dollars, and a season ticket for the Sydney Swans.

White Horse, Early Morning

Coming up through Meehan's field,
first light on a sea of white hoarfrost,

a shelter of old wood jammed against the hedge
and a barrel half-sunk by its own weight
in what once was mire.

Evil sometimes takes the form
of a white horse, the clink of chain –

my grandfather said, as he ripped
and burned the playing cards,

and kept me from sin,
caged in the chicken run:

the devil a black cockerel.

And a white horse stands in the mist,

muscle and flesh bearing down,
smelling of dung,

the metallic ring on hard ground,
eyes devoid of human understanding,

like my grandfather's, rolled back in death.

Stone

This stone house and outbuildings are buried into the hillside:
I watched him strain to lift stones that seemed then boulders,
yet he laid each one in place with the lightest touch.

He told me life and death are like Loughareema,
whose waters come and go, never more sure of himself
than when climbing Crocknacreeva to pen sheep.

And he could not understand the swelling in his belly –
three months I watched him wither on the bed
rising torturously to stare across the Issbawn,

until barely able to turn his head, he asked
who would finish the dry wall he had begun?

As though it alone could hold back
some quickening storm behind eyes already stone.

Baggy shapes are bent to the banks of moss,
the reverential echo of blade slicing between sullen mountains,
cars parked along one side of the road, like evening Mass.

On the day of his burial I looked out from Tievebulliagh
across Glenballyemon to Lurigethan and the sea at Red Bay.

We put into the land what we take out, he once said:
from this highland cairn I take down stone
to slot into the wall he could not finish.

In a Bombed Hotel in Portstewart

Schoolchildren huddle against the wind
on a rain-lashed promenade,
crows squawk from loose telegraph wires,

and here, in a bombed hotel in Portstewart
shoe soles crunch over gravel, cement,
minute fragments of shattered glass.

Pitted steps lead nowhere to an air-hungry doorway,
and the charred remains of a staircase
spiral through empty rooms to a sky cold with stars.

On the unscathed billboard out front
a handwritten poster advertises
the Friday dance – several seasons ago,

and the hollow black-rimmed windows are commonplace now,
like the ruins of a castle perched on a hill.

At night, there is a gap in the ring of town lights,
and a hundred empty caves for the wind to howl.

No one dresses for the new moon,
no one prepares a set supper in the kitchen.

Young waitresses pass ethereal with the local band,
and the bar staff stand eternal at their places.

Crossing

My great-grandfather was a migrant worker
taking the mailboat with men gathered along the North Coast
and crossing to Scotland, in his shoulder bag some bread, tobacco,
a bottle of water, cutthroat, and Bible.

On coaling vessels, he steam-trawled from Aberdeen
fishing the rich Faroese and Icelandic waters
his hands scarred with salt-sea and netting.

In Dundee he softened jute brought up the Tay
from Calcutta, Karachi, Bombay, with whale oil and water,
in Perth made calicoes and muslins,
canvas sails for the British navy made in Fife.

In the shipyards of the Clyde he hammered white-hot rivets
tossed by riveter boys on wooden scaffolding,
the clanging noise of iron splitting his eardrums.

Lodged in tenements without privies or drains,
a festering dunghill in the court –
spent his evening in the temperance halls.

Dreamed of going out to sheepfarm with a brother in Manawatu:
and when his first wife died spitting bloody sputum into a bowl,
he bought a young girl over from Glasgow to look after the children.

On the day the gun carriage, the standard over the coffin pall,
was pulled by sailors through streets decorated with purple and white,
my great-grandfather was laid to rest in falling snow
in a small churchyard in Benmore, looking out to the sea and Kintyre.

Return to Galway

After a silent supper at the crowded hotel in Tuam
(a tinker wedding party drunk and spilling into the summer evening)

we drove into the West and the light of a red sun,
the hum of the engine the only sound for miles.

And once I would have pointed out a sparrow hawk
circling high above the flat plain and raised bogs.

Back then, we would have taken the time, stopped the car,
a walk out across the moss, crunching over sundew, butterwort,
bell heather, or along walkways of wood or stone into the heart of it,

and sit in the stillness, picking out the cries of groundnesters –
skylark, curlew, snipe – as though we could tell the difference.

I am thinking of things that can never be the same,
and then the westerlies bring soft rain, and I lose the thread of it.

Is this the same hotel, or was it farther along the coast?
(twenty years is a jolting leap of time)

the young chambermaid with the armful of linen,
who disturbed us that morning on the bedroom floor.

Clabber Street

There is no respect for the condemned of Clabber Street,
like specimens under the microscope, here they are
their futile struggle against poverty for all to see
framed and mounted on this century's exhibition boards.

The narrow fetid alley of their lives, long demolished,
yet they exist forever in the eye of voyeurs who judge
and cannot equate disadvantage with ignorance and filth.

What sense have we that these were real houses?
not a straight jamb, window frame, or half-door,
the small bricks blackened by weather and running water.

And these tight-lipped women, how did they manage?
conception, birth, raising families, within these walls,
all washing done under the tap in the yard,
used flour-sacks for aprons, nappies, underwear.

This old woman on the iron-framed bed that fills the room
eyelids weighted with pennies, sunken chin tied-up with cotton,
and the laughing children vying for camera space at the flawed glass.

Here is the fishmonger with his salted ling and stone eye,
and here, men in sashes with a banner of an adorned Carson
(gaps in the kidney-shaped cobbles, the perfect form
for throwing at Catholics parading to chapel on Lady Day).

These young mill workers in crew necks and cloth caps
arms knotted, like a row of goalies, have left this image
while nothing of themselves remained in the pulverized fields of France.

Listen, we can hear the echo of children at play
with pig-bladder ball, wooden-crate pram, stuffed rag dolls,
and in this twilight, above the marble game at the alley end,
a line of aloof telegraph poles stretch to infinity.

Contrition

Our fathers were giants, loud voices in the home:
I would wait with a note for tick among the Mass-goers
queued for ice cream and cigarettes –

and Ireland was twenty miles up the line.

While my father in flapping dust coat seemed more enduring
than the massive beech that had blown across the road.

We were small prophets, mocking Gods,
cutting up live frogs in the timberyard.

The chosen, gathering beer-bottle caps on the waste ground
between the railway embankment and the tinker caravans.

Sunday-school bus trips coming back from the coast,
meandering down country roads to avoid stone throwers.

My father singing hymns with the television,
praising Monday and labour with bitter-sweet curses.

And now our extraordinary lives
have become ordinary in the thrall of great things –
marriage, parenthood, politics, deadend jobs:

my father's fear in a hospital bed.

And one ran screaming in a ploughed field, and fell,
a mouth full of blood and muck.

Thoughts on Armistice Day

The regimental badge will not stop the worm,
no more than the hens you longed for, and imagined
scratching on the stone slabs in the yard –

like throwing balls of bread at chickens
chalked on the barrack wall.

This one died by smoke,
lying semi-naked with another woman,
a wad of banknotes hidden in his underwear –
he would have taken his heroin to the grave, if able.

And if the dead converse in that other world
what understanding, or lack, between you?
or the woman passenger on her husband's motorcycle
who was elbowed off as they rounded a bend?

It isn't true that the best are taken –
death makes no distinction, either with the suffering wife,
the psychologically damaged child, or the violent husband.

Do the dead lambaste the living for this deceit of life?
if your blackened ashes had flaked the desert east of Cairo
what then, fifty years of petty cruelty?

To think of your bones without flesh or memory
holding the heavy settling clay – all underfoot, like hope:

no, we do not listen to the incoherence of the dying,
the awful meaning too clear – and the final process
that was there all along, for each of us just beginning.

Born Again

Here are the moon children,
hair the colour of barleycorn and bowl-cut round,
quaint neighbours in the townland of Carnalbanagh.

In puzzlement, they stand aloof in the schoolyard
holding hands, like paper dolls in homemade frocks –
their schoolwork always meticulous, if heavy with God.

The Antichrist is real among the broken farm implements,
the shreds of torn dress blowing in the hawthorns –
always at the elbow, he walks with Mass-goers.

In summer they hold baskets of washing for their mother to hang:
and Jacob is a small thing, all day wrestling in the bottom meadow –
the land is full of those who have turned from the Word.

They look at the antics of uncles, aunts, and cousins
with sadness in their large blue eyes,
who balk at grace round the table, unwashed in the blood of the lamb.

God is rather like their father – not to be crossed,
a dry love, silent and exact:
and sometimes at night, this tall house crashes in sin.

Testament

It was their truth, not mine
though I never questioned what was inbred,
an accepted and natural inevitability – like death.

That they were good men, I had no doubt,
hard-working, sometimes to the exclusion of all else,
yet I was slow to see the fault lines that was contradiction.

My great uncle, a guarded cobbler, mouth full of tacks,
cross-legged at the workshop window,
neither drank nor smoked, yet fathered three illegitimate children.

And my grandfather, whose everyday speech was biblical,
eschewing all that was underhand or false,
dutifully used his blockhammer like an ass's jawbone
on the unemployed Catholics outside the shipyard gate.

Their laws were clear, if not always just,
and need not be spoken to elicit fear,
like Jesus, who hung in every room,
they could see wrongdoing in a child's face.

And God spoke to them, a voice loud as their own,
never to the women, whose bodies harboured sin
(my cousin still bears the strap scars on her back
when he caught her playing with the iron poker).

My grandmother made us kneel and pray
while he was dying in the room above,
then took each of us in turn to pay our last respects.

And although the curtains were drawn on the living world,
with a child's horror I could clearly see
the black blood clotted in each nostril.

At her bidding, I kissed his parchment head
and with fascinated profanity, I whispered
into his cottonwool-plugged ear, Your God is dead.